ALL ABOUT ME

THE TEENAGE EDITION

ALSO BY PHILIPP KEEL

All About Me.

All About Me—Millennium Edition.

All About Us.

Look at Me

All About My Dog.

All About My Cat.

Technicolor

ALL ABOUT ME

THE TEENAGE EDITION

BY PHILIPP KEEL

BROADWAY BOOKS

NEW YORK

PRINTED IN THE UNITED STATES OF AMERICA

BROADWAY BOOKS and its logo, a letter B bisected on the diagonal, are trademarks of Random House, Inc.

Visit our website at www.broadwaybooks.com

First edition published 2004.

Based on an original design by Philipp Keel.

Cataloging-in-Publication Data is on file with the Library of Congress.

Thanks to Gabriela Kattan and Jeffrey Ray Wine.

ISBN 0-7679-1495-3

10 9 8 7 6 5 4 3 2 1

As you wander through the pages of this book, you will encounter various questions about your life and your state of mind. It is your choice how to use your *All About Me*. You can start from the beginning or you can randomly open to any page. You may decide to simply read it, or use it as a journal to record your thoughts. Either way, you will find out more about yourself and your relationships with others. And because it is a book, not a person, asking the questions, you can share whatever you are thinking and feeling. It can also be fun for you and your friends—or even your family—to playfully reveal your answers to one another.

However you choose to use *All About Me*, you will have the best experience if you try to answer spontaneously. If a question seems overwhelming don't struggle to answer it—just simply move on. Take it easy, remember that you'll never be young again. If you think it is hard being a teenager, wait until you are an adult.

This book is dedicated to my parents, Anna and Daniel, who dealt with me then and now.

—Philipp Keel

C O N T E N T S

I.D. *1*

Then *3*

Soon *5*

Favorites *13*

Money & Things *16*

Head Spin *21*

Knock Knock *24*

Opinions *27*

The Nest *30*

Friends *36*

Me *42*

What You Like *49*

What You Dislike *50*

Yes or No *51*

School *56*

1-800-Wishing *62*

Do Not Disturb *66*

Memories *70*

Another Chapter *74*

Fears & Doubts *76*

Sigmund *80*

Portrait *86*

Wonderland *87*

If *93*

Now *95*

ALL ABOUT ME

THE TEENAGE EDITION

Who are you? _____

How are you? _____

Your name: _____

If you don't like your name, what would you like to change it to? _____

Address: _____

Phone number: _____

Today's date: _____

Place of birth: _____

Date of birth: _____

Astrological sign: _____

Your current grade in school: _____

What would be better than school? _____

Height: _____

Weight: _____

Hair color: _____

Natural hair color: _____

Hair style: _____

Eye color: _____

Your favorite eye color: _____

Distinguishing marks: _____

You have a piercing or a tattoo.   ( ) Yes   ( ) No

If yes, what and where are they? _____

If no, what would you like to have?   ( ) Piercing   ( ) Tattoo   ( ) Both   ( ) Neither

What: _____

Where: _____

Blood type: _____

Allergies: _____

Your hobby: _____

Describe your personality in one word: _____

Describe your appearance in one word: _____

Your mother's full name: _____

Your mother's maiden name: _____

Her date of birth: _____

Something you envy about your mother's youth: _____

Your father's full name: _____

His date of birth: _____

Something you envy about your father's youth: _____

Your siblings' names and ages: _____

Do you wish you had more sisters or brothers?   ( ) Yes   ( ) No

If yes, why? _____

Grandparents on your mother's side: _____

Grandparents on your father's side: _____

Try to describe in one word or a sentence what your roots mean to you: _____

_____

Do you communicate with one of your relatives or grandparents
better than you do with your parents?   ( ) Yes   ( ) No

If yes, with whom? _____

Your mother's family comes from: _____

Your father's family comes from: _____

A famous or notable relative or ancestor: _____

( ) You don't really care about your family history.

Where will you be in the future? _____

Do you often think about the future?　　　　　　　　　　　　( ) Yes　　( ) No

If yes, what are you looking forward to? _____

If yes (again), what are you *not* looking forward to? _____

One goal you will probably reach in the future: _____

One goal you will probably not reach in the future: _____

One wish for the world in the future: _____

A social behavior that should be banned in the future: _____

A phrase or saying that should be banned in the future: _____

A product or brand that should be banned in the future: _____

An invention that would make your life easier: _____

Predictions for the future:

A McDonald's on the moon

　　　　( ) within 5 years.　( ) within 25 years.　( ) in the next century.　( ) never.

Cures for cancer and AIDS over the counter

　　　　( ) within 5 years.　( ) within 25 years.　( ) in the next century.　( ) never.

Empty highways

( ) within 5 years.   ( ) within 25 years.   ( ) in the next century.   ( ) never.

A third world war

( ) within 5 years.   ( ) within 25 years.   ( ) in the next century.   ( ) never.

Most people will live to be 125

( ) within 5 years.   ( ) within 25 years.   ( ) in the next century.   ( ) never.

Politicians truly serve the public

( ) within 5 years.   ( ) within 25 years.   ( ) in the next century.   ( ) never.

Relationships are easier

( ) within 5 years.   ( ) within 25 years.   ( ) in the next century.   ( ) never.

CD players are for sale only in antique stores

( ) within 5 years.   ( ) within 25 years.   ( ) in the next century.   ( ) never.

A limit of two children per family

( ) within 5 years.   ( ) within 25 years.   ( ) in the next century.   ( ) never.

Peace and prejudice are no longer issues

( ) within 5 years.   ( ) within 25 years.   ( ) in the next century.   ( ) never.

Africa is the richest continent

( ) within 5 years.   ( ) within 25 years.   ( ) in the next century.   ( ) never.

Most Americans speak more than one language

( ) within 5 years. ( ) within 25 years. ( ) in the next century. ( ) never.

Admission tickets are needed to visit the centers of world capitals

( ) within 5 years. ( ) within 25 years. ( ) in the next century. ( ) never.

Homosexuality is accepted in every society in the world

( ) within 5 years. ( ) within 25 years. ( ) in the next century. ( ) never.

Flowers, fruits, and vegetables grow overnight

( ) within 5 years. ( ) within 25 years. ( ) in the next century. ( ) never.

A woman, a rap or a pop star will be elected President

( ) within 5 years. ( ) within 25 years. ( ) in the next century. ( ) never.

Pet-sized elephants, giraffes, and zebras

( ) within 5 years. ( ) within 25 years. ( ) in the next century. ( ) never.

Contact with creatures from outer space

( ) within 5 years. ( ) within 25 years. ( ) in the next century. ( ) never.

Disney buys Egypt and turns it into a theme park

( ) within 5 years. ( ) within 25 years. ( ) in the next century. ( ) never.

Vegas goes bankrupt

( ) within 5 years. ( ) within 25 years. ( ) in the next century. ( ) never.

Wheel chairs have no wheels

( ) within 5 years.   ( ) within 25 years.   ( ) in the next century.   ( ) never.

Human waste is recycled into energy.

( ) within 5 years.   ( ) within 25 years.   ( ) in the next century.   ( ) never.

All races have completely mixed, to form one race

( ) within 5 years.   ( ) within 25 years.   ( ) in the next century.   ( ) never.

Plastic surgery is as common as getting a haircut

( ) within 5 years.   ( ) within 25 years.   ( ) in the next century.   ( ) never.

Life is beautiful

( ) within 5 years.   ( ) within 25 years.   ( ) in the next century.   ( ) never.

What comes to mind when you read the word "future"? _____

Your greatest achievement so far: _____

The kind of person you will most likely kiss sooner or later: _____

Do you plan on having children in the future?   ( ) Yes   ( ) No

If yes, why? _____

How many? _____

Do you believe that the pace of life in our society will slow down again?   ( ) Yes   ( ) No

If yes, what will it take to make that happen? _____

You believe that human beings are becoming

      ( ) more aware of themselves and others.   ( ) less aware of themselves and others.

What will change in the future?

Car dealers:	( ) Better	( ) Worse
World hunger:	( ) Better	( ) Worse
Holiday destinations:	( ) Better	( ) Worse
Manners:	( ) Better	( ) Worse
Pollution:	( ) Better	( ) Worse
Art and design:	( ) Better	( ) Worse
Communication:	( ) Better	( ) Worse
Health:	( ) Better	( ) Worse
Christmas or Hannukah:	( ) Better	( ) Worse
Unemployment rate:	( ) Better	( ) Worse
Parents:	( ) Better	( ) Worse
Product quality:	( ) Better	( ) Worse
Customer service:	( ) Better	( ) Worse
Fast food:	( ) Better	( ) Worse
Freedom:	( ) Better	( ) Worse

Movies: ( ) Better   ( ) Worse

Innocence: ( ) Better   ( ) Worse

Education: ( ) Better   ( ) Worse

Public bathrooms: ( ) Better   ( ) Worse

Toys: ( ) Better   ( ) Worse

News and radio people: ( ) Better   ( ) Worse

Something you would like to experience in the future: _____

_____

A recent fantasy you have had about the future: _____

_____

What will you most likely miss about the past? _____

_____

Do you believe the human race will end?   ( ) Yes   ( ) No

If yes, when? _____

Why? _____

Who will become the next Mozart? _____

What will replace oil? _____

What will the Internet cause? _____

What will replace the desire to explore the world? _____

What will be the consequences of cellular phones? _____

What will replace cigarettes (and such)? _____

What will be more important than environmental issues? _____

_____

What will replace weapons? _____

What will replace shaving? _____

What will replace the wish to be rich? _____

What will bring back tradition, quality, and style? _____

What will be memorable about the time you grew up? _____

_____

Do you believe you are one of the "future generation"?   ( ) Yes   ( ) No

If yes, what makes you and/or your generation so special? _____

_____

_____

What will always be on people's minds? _____

_____

FAVORITES

Your favorite thing to do: _____

Your favorite way to dress: _____

Your favorite person: _____

Your favorite animal: _____

A flower you really like: _____

A smell that you love: _____

A taste that is exciting: _____

Your favorite sport: _____

A city you would like to visit: _____

A country you would like to explore: _____

A famous person you would like to be: _____

Your favorite meal: _____

Your favorite drink: _____

A delicious desert: _____

Your favorite fantasy: _____

F A V O R I T E S

A game you like to play: _____

A book you strongly recommend: _____

The magazine you read most frequently: _____

A newspaper you occasionally enjoy: _____

Music you prefer to listen to when you are

      sad: _____

      happy: _____

      lovesick: _____

      getting ready to go out: _____

      lonely: _____

      angry (*or jealous*): _____

      with friends: _____

Your lucky number or symbol: _____

The movie you can watch over and over: _____

Your favorite musician or group: _____

F A V O R I T E S

An actress you admire: _____

An actor you admire: _____

A TV show you like to watch: _____

An artist whose work you like: _____

A monument or building you would like to have a view of from your bed: _____

_____

Your favorite time of day: _____

Your motto or your philosophy: _____

Your favorite place to sit at home: _____

What you most like to do on a free day: _____

The thing that makes you happiest: _____

Your favorite state of mind: _____

Your family is

    ( ) rich. ( ) doing very well. ( ) doing okay. ( ) "let's talk about something else."

You live in a

    ( ) mansion. ( ) nice house. ( ) modest house. ( ) apartment. ( ) mobile home.

Your family's car(s)

    ( ) is /are the best. ( ) is just a car/are just cars. ( ) is /are an embarrassment.

If you can drive, your car is

    ( ) your dream car. ( ) your first car. ( ) a piece of junk—but it works.

How often do you argue with your parents about money?

    ( ) All the time ( ) Sometimes ( ) Enough
    ( ) Never (*maybe they feel guilty about something*)

Your parents give you an allowance.   ( ) Yes ( ) No

If yes, how much is it? _____

How much should you get? _____

If you do receive an allowance, how does it make you feel? _____

_____

Your parents let you use one of their credit cards.   ( ) Yes ( ) No

If yes, do you take advantage of it?   ( ) Yes   ( ) No   ( ) Sometimes

Do you have a bank account?   ( ) Yes   ( ) No

What is the balance? _____

What should it be? _____

Have you ever received a large amount of money?   ( ) Yes   ( ) No

What was the reason (*inheritance, trust fund, bar/bat-mitzvah, etc.*)? _____

_____

How did having or receiving a large amount of money change your thinking? _____

_____

Whether or not you have money, you are

    ( ) almost too generous.   ( ) giving.
    ( ) conscious of getting your share.
    ( ) unfortunately a little stingy.

Are you discreet about your or your family's money?

    ( ) You were told to be.
    ( ) You've realized that it's smarter to keep those things quiet.
    ( ) It never was an issue.
    ( ) You enjoy showing off your family's wealth.
    ( ) You actually love to talk about money.

M O N E Y & T H I N G S

If your parents don't give you any money, what is the reason? _____

_____

Things you wish you could afford: _____

_____

Is there someone else who is helping you out with money
(*uncle, grandmother, friend, stranger*)?   ( ) Yes   ( ) No

Do your parents know about it?   ( ) Yes   ( ) No

If no, why is it a secret? _____

Do you have a job?   ( ) Yes   ( ) No

If yes, what is your job? _____

Hours per week: _____

Income per week: _____

The best part about your job: _____

The worst part about your job: _____

Do you like your job?   ( ) Yes   ( ) No

If no, what would you prefer to do? _____

In a perfect world, what would be your ideal career? _____

Material possessions are: _____

Your watch: _____ Your brand of shoes: _____

Your brand of clothing: _____ Your line of cosmetics: _____

Your cologne or perfume: _____

Status symbols are: _____

Something important in your room: _____

On your wall hangs: _____

If you had a safe, you would hide: _____

Things you like to buy: _____

Things your parents won't let you have: _____

Things you buy, regardless: _____

If you could afford it at this moment, you would buy: _____

You collect: _____

You don't have a lot of: _____

You have too many: _____

Your strangest possession: _____

Your most expensive possession: _____

Your most prized possession: _____

If you had to get rid of one thing, what would it be? _____

Money is

      ( ) extremely important. ( ) part of life. ( ) making everything easier.
      ( ) a constant hassle. ( ) the source of all imbalance and trouble in this world.

( ) Morals help you more often than not.   ( ) Morals restrict your freedom to explore.

Something forbidden you have done that might surprise even your closest friends: _____

_____

People should not marry before this age: _____

People should not have children before this age: _____

When something is your fault, you tend to

     ( ) tell a lie.   ( ) tell a white lie.   ( ) tell the truth.

Your most recent lie: _____

A lie you tell yourself: _____

A lie you have told others and wish you could take back: _____

Something you have stolen that was not worth the risk: _____

You owe someone money but have stalled in paying it back.   ( ) Yes   ( ) No

If yes, what is the reason? _____

When you have a curfew—and your parents have left for the evening,

( ) you are a good kid. ( ) you are afraid and turn music on.
( ) you invite your friends over. ( ) you sneak out after they leave.
( ) you snoop through your parents' belongings. ( ) it doesn't make a difference.

The worst thing you ever said to your parents: _____

The worst thought you ever had about your parents: _____

Have you ever hit someone?   ( ) Yes   ( ) No

If yes, why? _____

You have read someone's diary or gone through someone's private belongings
without permission.   ( ) Yes   ( ) No

If yes, which best describes your reason?

( ) Jealousy ( ) Distrust ( ) Curiosity
( ) You were asked by someone else to do it.

If yes, what did you discover? _____

What would your reaction be if your girlfriend or boyfriend cheated on you? _____

_____

You have cheated.   ( ) Yes   ( ) No

A time you hurt someone emotionally on purpose: _____

_____

Did you apologize?   ( ) Yes   ( ) No

If no, why not? _____

If you could have or do it all, what would you have or do first? _____

_____

Do you believe in God?   ( ) Yes   ( ) No

Try to describe what God is to you: _____

What religion were you raised with? _____

Do you practice this religion?   ( ) Yes   ( ) No

Do you plan on always practicing this religion?   ( ) Yes   ( ) No

Your most spiritual moment: _____

The last time you were in a house of worship: _____

Death is: _____

How do you picture the end of the world? _____

God has spoken to you.   ( ) Yes   ( ) No

If yes, what did God tell you? _____

You believe that most wars start because of religious conflicts.   ( ) Yes   ( ) No

If no, is it because people genuinely do not get along?   ( ) Yes   ( ) No

What did the first human being say to the second human being? _____

Do you believe in evolution?   ( ) Yes   ( ) No

If no, how did things get started? _____

_____

Do you believe in astrology?   ( ) Yes   ( ) No

If yes, why? _____

If you read your horoscope or spend $20 on a psychic, do you live by its or
his/her advice?   ( ) Yes   ( ) No

What is Karma? _____

If reincarnation does exist, you would like to come back as: _____

_____

If reincarnation had a bad day, you might come back as: _____

If your life was meant to be over right now,

    ( ) you would be sent to heaven.   ( ) you would be sent to hell.
    ( ) you would make a stopover in the middle.

One thing you have done that God would be proud of: _____

One thing you have done that God would not be proud of: _____

What could be your mission in this life? _____

What is holy to you? _____

Adults don't like teenagers.   ( ) Yes   ( ) No

The worst opinion adults have about young people: _____

( ) It's important to have opinions.   ( ) Who cares about opinions?

Which of the following are you in favor of?

The right to own guns:	( ) Pro	( ) Con
Nursing homes:	( ) Pro	( ) Con
The death penalty:	( ) Pro	( ) Con
Rights and services for illegal immigrants:	( ) Pro	( ) Con

What is your opinion on:

politicians _____

media hype _____

fast food _____

spring break _____

reality TV _____

the military _____

garbage and waste _____

Which of the above issue concerns you the most? _____

Regarding this issue, you have spent quite some time

    ( ) thinking and discussing. ( ) researching. ( ) taking action. ( ) simply enjoying.
    ( ) being very concerned. ( ) inventing solutions.

The first step toward resolving poverty: _____

The first step toward resolving racism: _____

The environmental issue that concerns you the most: _____

Do you believe a person is defined by what he or she does for a living?   ( ) Yes ( ) No

If yes, why? _____

In general, when it comes to politics you define yourself as

    ( ) not yet developed. ( ) conservative. ( ) extremely rebellious. ( ) "it's all good."
    ( ) liberal. ( ) moderate.

To whom do you hate to be compared? _____

To whom do you compare yourself? _____

The worst crime against humanity: _____

The worst political crime: _____

The minimum punishment for hurting children should be: _____

You would fight in a war if: _____

A strong opinion you had (*it can be something as simple as the dislike of cauliflower*), that has

suddenly changed: _____

How do your parents treat you? _____

When it comes to you, what is your parents'

      biggest worry: _____

      least worry: _____

A rule that you understand, but can't wait to outgrow: _____

The worst punishment your parents ever gave you: _____

( ) Your mother understands you more.   ( ) Your father understands you more.

Something you wish your parents would encourage more: _____

Something you wish your parents would advise you against: _____

One thing you like about your mother: _____

One thing you like about your father: _____

Which question felt easier to answer?   ( ) Mother   ( ) Father

Are your parents still married?   ( ) Yes   ( ) No

Do your parents use you as a "go-between"?   ( ) Yes   ( ) No

Whom do you resemble physically?   ( ) Mother   ( ) Father

A character trait and a physical trait you inherited from your mother:

    character trait: _____

    physical trait: _____

A character trait and a physical trait you inherited from your father:

    character trait: _____

    physical trait: _____

One thing you dislike about your mother: _____

One thing you dislike about your father: _____

Which question felt easier to answer?   ( ) Mother   ( ) Father

Something your mother does that embarrasses you: _____

Something your father does that embarrasses you: _____

When you were a child, your parents spent

    ( ) enough time with you.   ( ) not very much time with you.
    ( ) not enough time with you.   ( ) even the holidays without you.

You and your parents always argue about: _____

Your most beautiful childhood memory: _____

Two people that, if you didn't know your parents, you would choose as your mother
and your father:

Mother: _____

Father: _____

Two famous people that, if they were available, you would chose as your mother and your father:

Mother: _____

Father: _____

Do you think you say "I love you" enough to your mother?　　　( ) Yes　　( ) No

Do you think you say "I love you" enough to your father?　　　( ) Yes　　( ) No

Does your mother tell you that she loves you enough?　　　( ) Yes　　( ) No

Does your father tell you that he loves you enough?　　　( ) Yes　　( ) No

Your mother often says: _____

Your father often says: _____

Your parents fight

　　　( ) a lot.　( ) sometimes.　( ) discreetly.　( ) not enough.

Overall, the atmosphere in your house is

    ( ) pleasant. ( ) a circus. ( ) like a library. ( ) unpredictable.
    ( ) like nothing anyone has ever seen before.
    ( ) better than what I have experienced at my friends' homes.

You enjoy going out or on vacation with your family.   ( ) Yes   ( ) No

If not, what would it take to make it more enjoyable? _____

Something your parents did that you have never forgiven: _____

_____

What would it take for you to forgive them? _____

If you had to imagine your mother as an animal, she would be: _____

If you had to imagine your father as an animal, he would be: _____

You and your siblings share: _____

A trait you do not share with your siblings: _____

A trait or quality one of your siblings has that you are jealous of: _____

    Who: _____

    What: _____

If you are an only child, what is good about it? _____

What is not so good about it? _____

You wish you had   ( ) a brother.   ( ) a sister.

Why? _____

Your favorite relative is: _____

Why? _____

Your least favorite relative is: _____

Why? _____

If you were not related to your family members, you would still choose this one as your friend:

_____

Try to describe your parents' life in one sentence: _____

_____

What would it take for you to live your parents' life? _____

_____

Something you know your mother dreams about having or changing: _____

_____

Something you know your father dreams about having or changing: _____

_____

If your parents are divorced, with whom are you living?   ( ) Mother   ( ) Father   ( ) Both

What is most difficult for you about your parents' divorce? _____

_____

What changed for the better after your parents got divorced? _____

_____

Something you wish for your mother: _____

Something you wish for your father: _____

Something you wish for your sister(s) and/or brother(s)? _____

One thing you would never allow your children to do: _____

What does your family mean to you? _____

_____

F R I E N D S

How many friends do you have? _____

Three traits you look for in a friend:

1. _____

2. _____

3. _____

Who are your three best friends?

1. _____

2. _____

3. _____

One trait you admire about each of these three friends:

1. _____

2. _____

3. _____

One trait you wish each of them would change:

1. _____

2. _____

3. _____

The thing you enjoy doing the most with your friends: _____

The thing you enjoy doing the least with your friends: _____

Something you struggle with when you are with a group of friends: _____

A friend your parents don't approve of: _____

A friend whom you miss: _____

When did you last see this friend? _____

When do you think you will see this friend again? _____

A friend who makes you laugh: _____

A friend with whom you like to explore: _____

A friend to whom you can tell anything: _____

A friend to whom you can go for advice: _____

The best piece of advice this friend has given you: _____

_____

A friend you can go absolutely crazy with: _____

A friend you can flirt with: _____

A friend you should not flirt with as much as you do: _____

A friend you would like to kiss: _____

A friend you don't take seriously: _____

A friend you may lose soon: _____

Why? _____

A friend you have lost for a reason other than death: _____

    ( ) You would like to see this friend again.   ( ) You hope to never see this friend again.
    ( ) If you were to see this friend again, you would be unaffected.

A friend who does or believes in something you cannot respect: _____

Describe what it is that you cannot respect: _____

A friend with whom you would like to be closer: _____

Describe the barrier that exists between you and this friend: _____

F R I E N D S

A friend to whom you would never lend money: _____

Why? _____

A friend who has betrayed you: _____

How did this friend betray you? _____

Have you forgiven this friend?   ( ) Yes   ( ) No

A friend who has done something terrible, but whom you have forgiven: _____

Describe what you have forgiven: _____

A friend you need to forgive: _____

A friend to whom you have something important to say, but have not yet had the courage:

_____

What is it that you want to say? _____

Your mother is your friend.   ( ) Yes   ( ) No

Your father is your friend.   ( ) Yes   ( ) No

Your best friend as a child: _____

Your worst enemy as a child: _____

F R I E N D S

Someone you really dislike right now: _____

If you could, where would you banish this person? _____

Are you able to forgive your enemies?   ( ) Yes   ( ) No

If no, why not? _____

Does it ever occur to you that you might pick the wrong friends?   ( ) Yes   ( ) No

If yes, what general trait is missing in your current friendships? _____

A piece of advice about friendship that you will always remember: _____

The friend who is most like you: _____

Why? _____

The friend who is most unlike you: _____

Why? _____

What is a good friend? _____

Something a friend of yours experienced that you are jealous of: _____

_____

F R I E N D S

Something you have experienced that you know your friends would be jealous of: _____

_____

Something you wish you could tell your friends, but you are afraid what they might think of you:

_____

In a friendship,

( ) you tend to give more.   ( ) you tend to take more.

Considering all your friendships, you have learned this: _____

_____

M E

What you like most about yourself: _____

What you like least about yourself: _____

Who is your idol? _____

Why is this person your idol? _____

Your best quality (*even if it causes trouble*): _____

Your worst quality (*even if it works for you—and others*): _____

A recent time when this quality caused you problems: _____

_____

You consider yourself intelligent, but you can't make a paper airplane.   ( ) Yes   ( ) No

( ) Girls like me.   ( ) Boys like me.   ( ) Nobody likes me.

Three words that describe how others view you:

1. _____

2. _____

3. _____

Three words that you would use to describe your ideal self:

1. _____

2. _____

3. _____

Three things for which you are often complimented:

1. _____

2. _____

3. _____

Which one of the three is most meaningful to you?   ( ) 1   ( ) 2   ( ) 3

The best compliment you ever got: _____

Who gave you this compliment? _____

An insult that hurt you: _____

What was your reaction to this insult? _____

You are far better than most people you know at: _____

The animal that best describes you: _____

When you were five years old, you thought: _____

When you were ten years old, you thought: _____

What worries you now? _____

You are embarrassed when others: _____

Others are embarrassed when you: _____

The greatest amount of physical pain you have ever endured: _____

_____

The greatest amount of emotional pain you have endured: _____

_____

Your proudest moment: _____

Someone who shared this moment with you: _____

The moment you are most ashamed of: _____

Someone who shared this moment with you: _____

Your personality could be described as

    ( ) slow motion.   ( ) play.   ( ) fast forward.   ( ) high speed.

When describing your accomplishments to others, you tend to

( ) exaggerate.   ( ) understate.   ( ) be factual.

When telling stories or relaying the details of your day, you tend to

( ) exaggerate.   ( ) understate.   ( ) be factual.

Your best physical feature: _____

A physical feature you would like to change: _____

_____

Create a newspaper headline you would like to read about yourself: _____

_____

Complete the following with only one or two words:

You save _____

You kick _____

You have _____

You mind _____

You know _____

You wonder _____

You sing _____

You suffer _____

You love _____

You buy _____

You fear _____

You enjoy _____

You want _____

You hope _____

You pay _____

You expect _____

You dream _____

You assume _____

You neglect _____

You underestimate _____

You manipulate _____

You overestimate _____

You scream _____

You forget _____

You mean _____

You fulfill _____

You hate _____

You beg _____

You thank _____

You suspect _____

You distrust _____

You move _____

You risk _____

You maintain _____

You are _____

You really (*feel free to use more than one or two words here*) _____

_____

Your most recent selfless act: _____

The dumbest thing you ever did: _____

The most painful criticism you ever got: _____

_____

If you didn't have responsibilities to others, you would: _____

_____

Randomly list everything that comes to mind.

Randomly list everything that comes to mind.

You can make decisions.	( ) Yes	( ) No
You enjoy good food.	( ) Yes	( ) No
You care about your body.	( ) Yes	( ) No
You love talking on the phone.	( ) Yes	( ) No
You doodle while you are on the phone.	( ) Yes	( ) No
You are reliable.	( ) Yes	( ) No
You have read more than one book in the past month.	( ) Yes	( ) No
You replace the toilet-paper roll after using the last sheet.	( ) Yes	( ) No
You like comedy.	( ) Yes	( ) No
You consider yourself a happy person.	( ) Yes	( ) No
You have visited a place that changed your thinking.	( ) Yes	( ) No
You have a secret with someone that you can never share.	( ) Yes	( ) No
You always wait until the last minute (*you are always late*).	( ) Yes	( ) No
You like surprises.	( ) Yes	( ) No
You think you snore.	( ) Yes	( ) No
You talk too much.	( ) Yes	( ) No
You dislike confrontation.	( ) Yes	( ) No
You wish you were more organized.	( ) Yes	( ) No
You like the American way of life.	( ) Yes	( ) No
You wish you were older.	( ) Yes	( ) No

You have good manners.   ( ) Yes   ( ) No

You are extremely moody.   ( ) Yes   ( ) No

Foreign cultures scare you.   ( ) Yes   ( ) No

You read magazines in the bathroom.   ( ) Yes   ( ) No

Being sick feels like a vacation.   ( ) Yes   ( ) No

You don't like to have friends over at your parents' house.   ( ) Yes   ( ) No

You think education is a privilege.   ( ) Yes   ( ) No

You find many things quite annoying.   ( ) Yes   ( ) No

You can tell jokes.   ( ) Yes   ( ) No

You play games to kill time.   ( ) Yes   ( ) No

You like to observe people.   ( ) Yes   ( ) No

You feel awkward in public.   ( ) Yes   ( ) No

Your mother or father loves you too much.   ( ) Yes   ( ) No

You care about underwear.   ( ) Yes   ( ) No

You pray regularly.   ( ) Yes   ( ) No

You remember your dreams.   ( ) Yes   ( ) No

Sundays are boring.   ( ) Yes   ( ) No

You eat too fast.   ( ) Yes   ( ) No

You want to be wild, but you are not.   ( ) Yes   ( ) No

You know your parents well.   ( ) Yes   ( ) No

You need a lot.	( ) Yes	( ) No
You recycle.	( ) Yes	( ) No
You always think about the same stuff.	( ) Yes	( ) No
You drink enough water.	( ) Yes	( ) No
You like nature.	( ) Yes	( ) No
You are perceived as a "good kid."	( ) Yes	( ) No
You shave.	( ) Yes	( ) No
You are good at improvising.	( ) Yes	( ) No
You often get headaches.	( ) Yes	( ) No
A photograph or footage of you that no one should see exists.	( ) Yes	( ) No
You enjoy being photographed or filmed.	( ) Yes	( ) No
You can whistle.	( ) Yes	( ) No
You sometimes get sad and you don't know why.	( ) Yes	( ) No
Cellular phones and e-mail make everything more complicated.	( ) Yes	( ) No
You believe in destiny.	( ) Yes	( ) No
You walk around while you brush your teeth.	( ) Yes	( ) No
You have something you wish to confess.	( ) Yes	( ) No
You feel at home in your room.	( ) Yes	( ) No
You pick your nose.	( ) Yes	( ) No
You are living a healthy life.	( ) Yes	( ) No

You have traveled alone.   ( ) Yes   ( ) No

You have gone to a movie alone.   ( ) Yes   ( ) No

You can't stop biting your fingernails.   ( ) Yes   ( ) No

You are often ashamed of your thoughts.   ( ) Yes   ( ) No

You care about the news.   ( ) Yes   ( ) No

You care too much about your hair.   ( ) Yes   ( ) No

You lose control during arguments.   ( ) Yes   ( ) No

Your computer is your best friend.   ( ) Yes   ( ) No

Airplanes and hospitals make you nervous.   ( ) Yes   ( ) No

You have hit your father or mother in anger.   ( ) Yes   ( ) No

When you are wrong, you apologize.   ( ) Yes   ( ) No

You are addicted to Coca-Cola or chocolate or coffee.   ( ) Yes   ( ) No

You think about money all the time.   ( ) Yes   ( ) No

You get out of bed immediately.   ( ) Yes   ( ) No

You save things.   ( ) Yes   ( ) No

You are comfortable at parties.   ( ) Yes   ( ) No

You are afraid of guns.   ( ) Yes   ( ) No

You always have the last word.   ( ) Yes   ( ) No

You wish everyone cared more.   ( ) Yes   ( ) No

You have a hard time accepting things.   ( ) Yes   ( ) No

You think about those who have less.   ( ) Yes   ( ) No

You are popular.   ( ) Yes   ( ) No

Life treats you well.   ( ) Yes   ( ) No

You know who you are.   ( ) Yes   ( ) No

( ) School is harder than life.   ( ) Life is harder than school.

You are more comfortable   ( ) at home.   ( ) at school.

When you sit in school (*regardless of the class*), what is usually on your mind? _____

What do you get from school? _____

What does your school get from you? _____

Who is your favorite teacher? _____

What is it about her or him that you like? _____

Do you have a crush on her or him?   ( ) Yes   ( ) No

Your favorite subject: _____

Why is it your favorite subject? _____

In class, you are

      ( ) the teacher's pet.   ( ) the class clown.   ( ) popular.   ( ) teased, but liked.
      ( ) the hottest.   ( ) the dork or a nerd.   ( ) the "sensitive" one.
      ( ) "the "untouchable" one."   ( ) invisible.

( ) You pick your friends.   ( ) Your friends pick you.

You are part of a clique.   ( ) Yes   ( ) No

If yes, describe your clique in one word: _____

Why are you a member of this clique? _____

A club or an extracurricular activity you are involved in: _____

You add more challenges to your schedule

      ( ) because it is your choice.   ( ) because your parents make you.
      ( ) because you want to make your parents proud.
      ( ) because you are already thinking of your future.

When you are taking an exam

      ( ) you know what you are doing.   ( ) you try harder each time.
      ( ) you don't know what you are doing.   ( ) the teacher likes you, so you'll get by.
      ( ) you know, but you blank out.   ( ) you are counting the days until summer.
      ( ) you wonder how you'll make it to graduation.
      ( ) you are unconsciously hoping to flunk out.

You occasionally cheat.   ( ) Yes   ( ) No

You are resentful of those who do not need to cheat.   ( ) Yes   ( ) No

Your technique for cheating (*if you don't cheat, make one up*): _____

If you have been caught cheating, what was the punishment? _____

If your parents found out, what were the consequences? _____

If you have ever had a serious disciplinary meeting at your school,

what effect did it have on you? _____

Have you ever been suspended?   ( ) Yes   ( ) No

If yes, why? _____

Regardless of how you act, do you receive special treatment in school?   ( ) Yes   ( ) No

If yes, why? _____

A dream about school that haunts you: _____

Someone from your school whom you think about when you are not at school: _____

_____

A feeling that overcomes you when you leave school: _____

A feeling you have when you are not in school (*after hours, weekends, and holidays*): _____

_____

One thing you hide in your locker: _____

A strange thing your best friend hides in her or his locker: _____

One thing you would post in your locker if you were the opposite sex: _____

_____

An embarrassing moment in school that you relive over and over again: _____

_____

A time when you made a fool of yourself that no one lets you forget: _____

_____

A situation when you were a hero (*if there wasn't one, that's fine*): _____

_____

Something unexpected that happened one day at school: _____

_____

If you are not required to wear a uniform, how important is being in style at your school?

    ( ) It's everything.   ( ) Some can afford it, some can not.   ( ) We are all the same.
    ( ) Who cares?

If all goes well, your next step after school will be

    ( ) an Ivy League school.   ( ) a respectable college.
    ( ) the only school that accepts you.   ( ) a good job.   ( ) social work for a while.
    ( ) life experience.   ( ) taking a break.   ( ) marriage.   ( ) other:

Someone in your class who

    smells bad: _____

    annoys everyone: _____

will make it: _____

won't make it: _____

tortures you: _____

is odd: _____

is really crazy (*but nice*): _____

probably a pioneer: _____

affected you: _____

you feel sorry for: _____

helps everyone: _____

needs to get a life: _____

is privileged: _____

is not going to live very long: _____

is a sort of a genius: _____

needs a little more luck: _____

is just nice: _____

Your least favorite person in school: _____

Someone at your school whom you admire: _____

Someone you have teased: _____

How did you feel afterward? _____

Pick one:

      ( ) Your parents believe in your abilities.
      ( ) Your teachers believe in your abilities.
      ( ) You believe in your abilities.
      ( ) No one believes in you (*and therefore you will make it*).

What are wishes for? _____

( ) You have wishes.   ( ) You deny your wishes.   ( ) You express your wishes.
( ) You wish you could express your wishes.   ( ) You know—you don't need to wish.

You wish people treated you better.   ( ) Yes   ( ) No

You wish you treated people better.   ( ) Yes   ( ) No

A present you wish you could throw away, but you can't: _____

Your most secret wish: _____

If you had the talent or the opportunity, you would: _____

Something you wish you could learn with the snap of your fingers: _____

Something you wish you could change about your life today: _____

_____

Something you wish you could change about yourself without your family and closest friends

commenting on it: _____

You wish you had been born into a different race.   ( ) Yes   ( ) No

You wish you had been born into a different religion: _____ ( ) Yes   ( ) No

Someone's diary you would love to read: _____

A quality an ideal woman should possess: _____

A quality an ideal man should possess: _____

A quality an ideal relationship should have: _____

Something you wish you didn't need to discuss anymore at this age: _____

How would you like to spend the last minutes of your life? _____

If your last dinner was tomorrow, you would invite these three people:

1. _____

2. _____

3. _____

The menu for your last dinner would be

      appetizer: _____

      main course: _____

      dessert: _____

At your funeral, you want people to remember you as: _____

Someone who should not, under any circumstances, speak at your funeral: _____

What should it say on your tombstone? _____

A dream you often have that features the same wish: _____

Something you dreamed that later happened or turned out to be true: _____

Your most nasty wish: _____

A wish it would be better to not express: _____

You wish you were somewhere else right now.   ( ) Yes   ( ) No

       Where: _____

       With whom: _____

You wish you could always have fun.   ( ) Yes   ( ) No

If yes, what is fun to you? _____

A person who wishes something from you:

       Who: _____

       What: _____

Something impossible you wish from someone else:

       Who: _____

What: _____

Something you wished for, you got, and you now regret: _____

Why do you regret this wish? _____

You wish you never hurt your parents.   ( ) Yes   ( ) No

You wish no one ever got hurt.   ( ) Yes   ( ) No

If you have a pet, do you wish it could talk to you?   ( ) Yes   ( ) No

If yes, what advice would your pet give you? _____

What is your greatest wish? _____

If you could be granted your greatest wish, which positive aspect of your life would you be willing

to give up? _____

What is the opposite of a wish? _____

You wish you could understand more.   ( ) Yes   ( ) No

If yes, what makes you believe there is more to understand? _____

_____

The number one emotion: _____

The least important emotion: _____

The emotion you tend to hide the most: _____

An emotion you can't hide: _____

An emotion you would like to slap in the face: _____

The emotion you seem to experience the most: _____

The predominant emotion you have experienced lately: _____

A moment when you achieved absolute happiness: _____

_____

A moment in which you sensed your innocence: _____

_____

You have a great amount of guilt regarding: _____

_____

You would feel envious right now if: _____

A piece of music that touches you: _____

This music reminds you of: _____

When you want to be happy, you need: _____

When you are sad, you need: _____

When you are angry, you need: _____

When you are in love, you need: _____

When you are lonely, you need: _____

You would love it if someone told you: _____

The last time you were very angry with yourself: _____

_____

The last time you cried uncontrollably: _____

_____

The last time you laughed uncontrollably: _____

_____

If your problems were overwhelming, who would you ask for help? _____

A moment in your life when your emotions froze and you felt absolutely nothing: _____

_____

Someone who genuinely makes or has made you happy: _____

Something that makes you happy: _____

Something that or someone who makes you emotional: _____

You get angry with yourself when you: _____

Spontaneously match the following emotions with a color:

     Fear: _____

     Love: _____

     Happiness: _____

     Sadness: _____

     Anger: _____

     Guilt: _____

     Jealousy: _____

     Loneliness: _____

What is your favorite color? _____

When you feel excited

( ) nothing stops you.   ( ) you still look before you leap.   ( ) you just do.
( ) you obsess.   ( ) you don't know.

You are always embarrassed when you are (*use one word*): _____

You always feel ashamed when you try to (*use one word*): _____

You are always bored when you are (*use one word*): _____

What do you fear the most? _____

What do you fear the least? _____

When you are melancholic or frustrated about not being an adult yet, how do you like to cheer

yourself up? _____

How do you deal with your emotions? _____

Ideally, how would you like to deal with your emotions? _____

MEMORIES

Your earliest memory: _____

When you were a child, you believed: _____

Do you still believe this?   ( ) Yes   ( ) No

Your first kiss:

      When: _____

      Where: _____

      With whom: _____

The first time you fell in love:

      When: _____

      Where: _____

      With whom: _____

The last time your heart was broken: _____

Who helped you fix it? _____

Your most precious childhood memory: _____

A scary moment you cannot forget: _____

Something that makes you laugh whenever you think of it: _____

A person who was especially kind to you: _____

A person who made you miserable for a long time: _____

The most peaceful time of your life: _____

Your happiest birthday: _____

( ) You are better at remembering names.   ( ) You are better at remembering faces.

A tragic moment that has shaped you: _____

The most shocking experience that you ever had: _____

_____

A situation that taught you something for life: _____

_____

Something you wish you hadn't witnessed: _____

_____

Something you wish you had never heard: _____

_____

Something forbidden you did that you would like to do again (*don't be shy*): _____

( ) You are better at holding grudges.   ( ) You are too kind to not forgive.

A battle in your mind that you wish would disappear: _____

_____

A moment when your parents were truly in love: _____

_____

A moment when you feared your parents were splitting up: _____

_____

At that moment, you wished for this person to take care of you: _____

Your most jealous moment: _____

Your angriest moment: _____

A situation when you got rebellious: _____

One of your most desperate moments: _____

Someone you wish you had never met: _____

Someone you met who you would like to meet again: _____

Your most passionate moment: _____

A smell that reminds you of your childhood: _____

An object you still own or remember vividly from your childhood: _____

A routine you remember from your childhood: _____

You seem to deal most

( ) with yesterday.   ( ) with today.   ( ) with tomorrow.   ( ) NOT.

You sometimes wish you could be a baby again.   ( ) Yes   ( ) No

If yes, why? _____

A memory that will affect your whole life: _____

_____

( ) Sunrise or ( ) sunset.

( ) Sahara or ( ) Himalaya.

( ) Old or ( ) new.

( ) Soft or ( ) hard.

( ) Train or ( ) plane.

( ) Right now or ( ) a little later.

( ) Fast or ( ) slow.

( ) Blind or ( ) deaf.

( ) Woman or ( ) man.

( ) Earthquake or ( ) tornado.

( ) Vanilla or ( ) chocolate.

( ) One or ( ) more.

( ) Briefs or ( ) boxers.

( ) Today or ( ) tomorrow.

( ) Horizontal or ( ) vertical.

( ) Sweet or ( ) sour.

( ) Dolphin or ( ) eagle.

( ) Coca-cola or ( ) Mountain Dew.

( ) ! or ( ) ?

( ) Sun or ( ) moon.

( ) Orange or ( ) purple.

( ) Rap or ( ) pop.

( ) Written or ( ) spoken.

( ) Carpet or ( ) hardwood floor.

( ) City or ( ) countryside.

( ) Painting or ( ) photography.

( ) House or ( ) apartment.

( ) Pen or ( ) pencil.

( ) Summer or ( ) winter.

( ) Destiny or ( ) choice.

( ) Alone or ( ) together.

( ) Silver or ( ) gold.

( ) E-mail or ( ) letter.

( ) Poker or ( ) Tarot cards.

( ) Catalog or ( ) store.

( ) Library or ( ) Internet.

( ) Discovery Channel or ( ) MTV.

( ) Bored or ( ) stressed.

( ) Frisbee or ( ) boomerang.

( ) Cellular phone or ( ) land line.

( ) Serious or ( ) easy.

( ) Blue sky or ( ) rain.

( ) Theme park or ( ) park.

( ) Others or ( ) yourself.

( ) Gym or ( ) hiking.

( ) Doing the dishes or ( ) vacuuming.

( ) Religion or ( ) meditation.

( ) Pets or ( ) kids.

( ) Either or ( ) neither.

( ) Messy or ( ) neat.

F E A R S & D O U B T S

A positive aspect of having anxiety, fear, and doubts: _____

Which of these three feelings seem to overcome you most frequently? _____

In what situations do these feelings arise? _____

_____

Things you fear:

( ) Failure   ( ) Water   ( ) Parties   ( ) Spiders or snakes   ( ) Bullies
( ) Ceremonies   ( ) Injections   ( ) Highways   ( ) Dogs   ( ) The night
( ) Tests   ( ) Responsibility   ( ) Perverts   ( ) Concerts   ( ) Sirens
( ) Heartbreak   ( ) Knives   ( ) Doctors and dentists   ( ) Elevators   ( ) Heights
( ) Underground spaces   ( ) Police   ( ) Getting older   ( ) Rejection   ( ) Illness
( ) Fire   ( ) Getting caught   ( ) Almost everything   ( ) Other: _____

Your greatest fear: _____

Your most fearful moment: _____

A crime or a catastrophe (*or a natural disaster*) that you were a victim of: _____

_____

A sickness or disease you fear for a certain reason: _____

Why? _____

Your greatest fear about aging: _____

FEARS & DOUBTS

When people first meet you, you are afraid they will think: _____

A country you fear visiting: _____

Your greatest fear about marriage: _____

Your greatest fear about having children: _____

Something on your mind that you are afraid to share: _____

A plan or project you worry may fail: _____

Now, measure your fears:

Pet a snake.

    ( ) You did.   ( ) You would.   ( ) You would not.

Spend a week in an empty room.

    ( ) You did.   ( ) You would.   ( ) You would not.

Bungee-jumping off a 400-foot-high bridge.

    ( ) You did.   ( ) You would.   ( ) You would not.

Kill a good-sized animal.

    ( ) You did.   ( ) You would.   ( ) You would not.

Sky dive.

    ( ) You did.   ( ) You would.   ( ) You would not.

Perform in front of a huge audience.

( ) You did.   ( ) You would.   ( ) You would not.

Volunteer in a disease-ridden place.

( ) You did.   ( ) You would.   ( ) You would not.

Dramatically change your hairstyle.

( ) You did.   ( ) You would.   ( ) You would not.

Help to deliver a baby.

( ) You did.   ( ) You would.   ( ) You would not.

Swim across the Amazon River.

( ) You did.   ( ) You would.   ( ) You would not.

Run naked through your neighborhood.

( ) You did.   ( ) You would.   ( ) You would not.

Disappear for a long period of time.

( ) You did.   ( ) You would.   ( ) You would not.

Walk through a forest alone at night.

( ) You did.   ( ) You would.   ( ) You would not.

Join a space mission.

( ) You did.   ( ) You would.   ( ) You would not.

Tell everyone what you honestly think of them.

( ) You did.   ( ) You would.   ( ) You would not.

Pretend to rob a store or a bank.

( ) You did.   ( ) You would.   ( ) You would not.

Walk up to a street gang and call them names.

( ) You did.   ( ) You would.   ( ) You would not.

Disarm a bomb.

( ) You did.   ( ) You would.   ( ) You would not.

Clean the outside windows of a skyscraper.

( ) You did.   ( ) You would.   ( ) You would not.

Draw a mustache on the *Mona Lisa* with a permanent marker.

( ) You did.   ( ) You would.   ( ) You would not.

Eat a sandwich at a funeral.

( ) You did.   ( ) You would.   ( ) You would not.

Who needs psychology? _____

Do you ever think that you might need therapy? _____

How does that make you feel? _____

What is guilt? _____

( ) You feel guilty.   ( ) You rarely feel guilty.

Grade your self-confidence:

    ( ) Good.   ( ) Average.   ( ) Okay.   ( ) Fine.   ( ) Bad.   ( ) Terrible.

Grade your self-esteem:

    ( ) Amazing.   ( ) Alright.   ( ) Fair.   ( ) So-so.   ( ) Difficult.   ( ) Yuck.

A recurring dream that sends you a message: _____

_____

One thing you do exactly like your mother: _____

_____

One thing you do exactly like your father: _____

_____

You wish you never had to share your parents.   ( ) Yes   ( ) No

What seems to work best for you?

( ) Aggression   ( ) Anger   ( ) Frustration   ( ) Bitterness   ( ) Self-pity
( ) Sadness   ( ) Self-destruction   ( ) Insanity   ( ) "Don't go there."

A neurosis that you experience when you are

getting ready: _____

pressured: _____

socializing: _____

eating: _____

flirting: _____

purchasing: _____

relaxing: _____

A sound that drives you crazy: _____

A person who you fascinate: _____

Something you heard that makes you wonder: _____

Something you did that makes you uncomfortable: _____

Something you experienced that made you stronger: _____

Something you forced that you now wish you hadn't: _____

You are too young for: _____

You will always be too sensitive for: _____

At the moment, you are confused.   ( ) Yes   ( ) No

If yes, what is confusing you most? _____

You make bad judgments.   ( ) Yes   ( ) No

If yes, how can you make better judgments? _____

_____

You feel unloved when:

      ( ) no one calls you on your birthday
      ( ) your friends laugh without you
      ( ) your clothes don't fit
      ( ) one of your parents doesn't say good morning
      ( ) you are looking in the mirror
      ( ) your teacher points at you
      ( ) one of your siblings or relatives gets complimented
      ( ) people say "you are still young."

Your most romantic thought: _____

( ) There is one way.   ( ) There are many ways.

How do you feel when you hear your own voice? _____

How do you feel when you see your picture? _____

You would rather be

      ( ) a child again.   ( ) an adult soon.

Explain why you made your selection: _____

What confuses you about your identity? _____

One thing your parents find strange about you being a teenager: _____

One thing you find strange about your parents now that you are older: _____

You say thank you enough.   ( ) Yes   ( ) No

You can laugh at yourself.   ( ) Yes   ( ) No

You are being raised by someone other than your mother and father.   ( ) Yes   ( ) No

If yes, what have you gained that others can't know? _____

_____

You exaggerate when you are expressing youself.   ( ) Yes   ( ) No

You choose to speak in a way that you think makes you sound better.   ( ) Yes   ( ) No

You think you look better with a tan.   ( ) Yes   ( ) No

A special time when your mother felt like your closest friend: _____

_____

A special time when your father felt like your closest friend: _____

_____

A time when you needed your parents and they were not available: _____

_____

In general,

    ( ) you wish your parents were around more often.
    ( ) you enjoy it when your parents are not around that often.

Do you ever tell your parents that you need them?   ( ) Yes   ( ) No

You are

    ( ) a normal teenager.   ( ) not the normal teenager.   ( ) one of a kind.
    ( ) not a teenager, because life has made you older than your years.

Something that has been on your mind lately: _____

Something that has been on your mind for a long time: _____

A period in your life when you felt truly protected: _____

A period of time when you felt unprotected: _____

The first time you discovered power: _____

The person who has affected you the most: _____

What can you probably change about yourself? _____

What can you probably not change about yourself? _____

P O R T R A I T

(Even if you don't think you can draw well, spontaneously create a self-portrait here)

ALL ABOUT ME

Describe yourself when you have a crush in one word: _____

Do you easily develop crushes?   ( ) Yes   ( ) No

If no, what usually holds you back? _____

When someone has a crush on you,

    ( ) you are so surprised that you jump into their arms.
    ( ) you feel flattered, but you are shy.   ( ) you pull back.
    ( ) you act arrogant.
    ( ) you never realize it.

When you are attracted to someone,

    ( ) you like to be the cat.   ( ) you like to be the mouse.

A physical trait you find attractive: _____

An intellectual ability that you find attractive: _____

A personality trait that you find attractive: _____

The physical feature that you are most often complimented on: _____

_____

What is the most embarrassing thing about you or your life that you fear will be revealed once

someone gets to know you better: _____

A piece of advice your mother or father (*or both*) gave you about love, dating, and relationships

that you agree with: _____

A piece of advice your mother or father (*or both*) gave you about love, dating, and relationships

that you disagree with: _____

When you are at home alone you would love for this person to climb through your

bedroom window: _____

Someone who visits your house who is not allowed to visit: _____

Why is this person not allowed to visit you? _____

If you are not into dating, how do you prefer to spend your time? _____

How would you ideally spend your time with your dream date? _____

_____

In social situations, you tend to

( ) introduce yourself first.   ( ) wait for others to introduce themselves.

When you really want to get to know someone, you say or ask: _____

_____

What did you feel when you kissed someone for the first time? _____

_____

Your most romantic experience: _____

_____

A person you successfully pursued in a short amount of time: _____

A person you successfully pursued over a long period of time: _____

A person who unsuccessfully pursued you: _____

A person you unsuccessfully pursued: _____

Something someone said or did you found very attractive: _____

_____

Something someone said or did you found quite unattractive: _____

_____

Have you ever had a secret admirer?   ( ) Yes   ( ) No

One thing that is appealing about women: _____

One thing that is not appealing about women: _____

One thing that is appealing about men: _____

One thing that is not appealing about men: _____

A fragrence that reminds you of someone you have a crush on: _____

Your friends tend to be

      ( ) male.   ( ) female.   ( ) older than you.   ( ) younger than you.
      ( ) the same age.

Something you recently saw on TV that you would like to do on a date: _____

_____

If you are a girl, how does your father deal with your boyfriends? _____

_____

If you are a guy, how does your mother deal with your girlfriends? _____

_____

You are irritated when a date asks you: _____

You love it when a date asks you: _____

Your longest grudge against someone you dated: _____

When was the first time you learned about sex? _____

_____

You believe it is possible to be with one person for the rest of your life.   ( ) Yes   ( ) No

If no, what makes you skeptical about this concept? _____

_____

Something romantic that happened during a holiday that you will never forget: _____

_____

Something that happened during a party that you regretted the next day: _____

_____

You regret that you never had a relationship with this person: _____

What makes you think this person would have been worth it? _____

_____

A type of person you don't seem to get along with: _____

_____

The star sign you are most compatible with: _____

The star sign you are least compatible with: _____

When you are in a relationship, you argue about this issue often: _____

_____

In your relationships

( ) you seem to make most of the decisions.   ( ) you do not seem to make decisions.

The biggest risk you would take to be with someone you desire: _____

_____

The biggest risk you took to be with someone you desired: _____

_____

What you like about being in a relationship: _____

What you dislike about being in a relationship: _____

What is crazier than love? _____

If love is the answer, what is the question? _____

If love was a candy bar, which would it be? _____

You feel most attractive when: _____

A fantastic kisser: _____

How important is all this at this point in your life? _____

What else is as beautiful as being in love? _____

If you had more time alone, you would: _____

If you could ask your parents, or the person who is responsible for you, for a favor you already

know they won't fulfill, it would be: _____

If you could ask the President for a personal favor, it would be: _____

If you were the President, _____

If you could change anything about the world, _____

If you had a plane ticket to anywhere in the world, you would visit: _____

If you could live anywhere in the world, you would live in: _____

If you could visit any time period, you would chose: _____

If you could ask God one question, it would be: _____

If you could only pick one of the following for your life, you would choose

    ( ) to make people laugh.   ( ) to capture what you see.
    ( ) to teach what you know best.   ( ) to share your thoughts.
    ( ) to motivate others to reach a goal.   ( ) to be in control.   ( ) to be famous.
    ( ) to help.   ( ) to serve.   ( ) to not work.

If you could be famous, you would like to be famous for: _____

If you could, you would spend time with this famous person: _____

If you were stranded on a desert island, you would want this person with you: _____

_____

If you could change one rule, _____

If you were in prison, you would spend your time: _____

If you could erase one memory, _____

If you had extra money, _____

If you had all the money in the world, _____

If you could bring back one person from the dead, _____

If you had wings, you would fly above: _____

If you couldn't express yourself, _____

If you didn't have to learn anything about life, _____

If you could start all over, _____

Your ideal fortune cookie says: _____

Your current state of mind: _____

A beginner is a winner.   ( ) Yes   ( ) No

Something good that happened today: _____

Something that you have now that you will never have again: _____

What occupies your thoughts right now? _____

Something you learned recently: _____

Something you need to learn: _____

The person who has the greatest influence on you: _____

Your greatest challenge: _____

A major obstacle: _____

The word that best describes your life: _____

What would be a nice relief? _____

Your attitude toward yourself: _____

The last thing that confused you: _____

You are happier today than in the past. ( ) Yes ( ) No

The most important thing in your life: _____

The person who helps to compensate for your limitations: _____

A piece of wisdom you would pass on to a child: _____

Now that you have answered all the questions in *All About Me*, write one more question you

would like to answer: _____

The answer to your question is: _____

_____

( ) You wish you knew.   ( ) You are glad you don't.

You are, and therefore you say: _____

N O T E S

NOTES

ALL ABOUT ME

N O T E S

NOTES

ALL ABOUT ME